Who's on the Dance Music Tonight?

1945 - 1970

Acknowledgements

I make grateful acknowledgement to many people for their assistance in compilation of this book and make special mention of Ian Holmes, Bobby Crowe, Jack Cooper, Farquhar Mathieson, Dan Kerr and my son Alan.

ISBN 1 872350 67 4

to re-order this book contact the author:
James L. Helm,
1 Westfield Road,
Ayr. KA7 2XN
Tel: 01292 262379

Published by:
GC Book Publishers Ltd.
The Book Shop, 17 North Main Street,
Wigtown, Wigtownshire
SCOTLAND DG8 9HL
Tel/Fax: 01988 402499
sales@gcbooks.demon.co.uk
www.gcbooks.demon.co.uk

Printed and bound in Great Britain by
MPG Books Ltd, Bodmin, Cornwall

Who's on the Dance Music Tonight?

1945 - 1970

by

James L. Helm

I wish to dedicate this book to
my wife Nettie
for her patience and encouragement
throughout its compilation.

Contents

<u>Introduction</u>

James L. Helm, the author of this book was born at Ardentinny near Dunoon and educated at Strone School and Dunoon Grammar School.

His initial interest in Scottish Dance Music began during his latter schooldays when Scottish Country Dances were started locally. In 1956, with his brother Tom and friend Johnnie Peel, the Barnacabber Ceilidh Band was formed. Jimmy's employment in the agricultural business took him to reside in different parts of rural Scotland and, when in Wigtownshire in the 1970's, he played in the Alan Paterson Trio from Newton Stewart and was Secretary of the Stranraer Accordion and Fiddle Club.

The Barnacabber Ceilidh Band

The Barnacabber Ceilidh Band was formed in 1956 and played in Dunoon and the surrounding areas. They played in hotels during the summer season, local dances and for the Cowal Scottish Country Dance Club. The line up was:

Tom Helm - Accordion
Jimmy Helm - Second Accordion
Ian Barr - Violin
Jean Polson (followed by Helen Garrity) - Piano
Johnnie Peel - Drums

Tom left the band in 1958. His place was taken by Peter McFarlane, a fine young accordionist from Dunoon. A year later, Jimmy had to give up playing as a change of work took him away from the Dunoon district and his seat in the band was taken by Sammy George, a very talented and experienced player who had played in the David Hughes band from Dunoon.

The Barnacabber Ceilidh Band continued playing into the early sixties.

Left to right: Johnnie Peel (Drums), Tom Helm (Lead Accordian),
Jimmy Helm (2nd Accordian), Jean Polson (Piano)

THE BARNACABBER CEILIDH BAND.

Shall we dance a lively polka,
  See how good it makes you feel,
Or it could be a waltz or foxtrot,
  Ev'n a rousing eightsome reel!

If it's rhythm you are after
  Jimmy Helm supplies the beat,
When they play you feel like dancing,
  However young or old your feet,

Let it be the Dashing Sergeant,
  Or a barn dance (Canadian style),
You will find the music tempting,
  'Twill the coldest heart beguile.

But when they play the Island music,
  Tunes that have the heather tang,
Tunes that seem to beckon to you,
  Tunes that countless mothers sang,

Then the feet start really dancing,
  As though they were equipped with
    wings,
How they foot the lively measure,
  What a joy the music brings.

So, shall we dance a stately measure,
  More befitting to our age?
Or will we whoop it up with gusto,
  Like clansmen on a wild rampage.
                              Christabel.

A Newpaper Cutting taken from Dunoon's local paper, the Standard
in 1957. This was contributed by an unknown admirer of the band
called Christabel.

Page 9

Preface

Having been much involved in the golden days of the Scottish Dance Band, I'm delighted to preface Jimmy Helm's book.

He has taken so much trouble to depict an era when Scottish dance band musicians were household names in a world of broadcasting, recording, concerts and dances, with huge audiences for the thrice weekly radio programmes. The "On Tour" radio series, Radio 2 Ballroom and of course television featured "White Heather Club" and "The Kilt is my Delight". Dancers flocked the length and breadth of Scotland and indeed, into many areas South of the Border, to dance to their favourite musicians who they listened to on radio.

Record companies vied for the signatures of Bands to grace their labels - the halcyon days of our traditional music.

While the audiences have grown older, the melodies most certainly linger on.

Jimmy Helm has so adequately remembered those times - I wish his book every success.

Jim MacLeod
Stakis Dunblane Hotel
June, 1998.

Jim MacLeod

Who's on the Dance Music Tonight?
1945 - 1970

This is a book written to pay tribute to the many musicians who took part in what must have been the greatest period in Scottish dance music.

The world had just emerged from six years of darkness during the Second World War and a new social pattern was developing in which dancing was to play a great part.

Scottish country dancing became the 'in' thing with the young and old alike and country dance clubs sprang up in towns and villages throughout Scotland and in some parts of England. Old time and modern dancing was equally as popular and village halls could have two or three dances a week, so great was the demand and the desire of everyone to dance.

This desire for dancing provided a great opportunity for musicians to form bands and, with the BBC broadcasting Scottish dance music three times a week, a further interest in the Scottish dance scene was created. The top band leaders at that time were the pop stars of that era.

"Who's on the dance music tonight?", was a question often asked by dance music enthusiasts during the period from 1945 to 1970 and I'm sure to this day some may still ask it.

To be a musician in one of the prominent broadcasting bands

during the 40's and 50's was a very demanding life. A band could be playing in the Borders on a Friday night and be performing in Inverness or Wick the following evening. This was a very long journey indeed, as the road network throughout the country at that time was nothing like that which exists today. There were no motorways and the road surfaces were in a poor state of repair having had very little maintenance during the war years, hence a journey could take twice as long at least. Transport was another problem. There were no new cars around, only pre war ones, many of which had been mothballed during the war, and their reliability was questionable. Petrol was still rationed. However, despite these obstacles, bands were seldom late for an engagement, such was their enthusiasm.

Many of the outlying villages throughout the country at that time had no electricity. There was no amplification, and tilley lamps provided the illuminations. The objective of the musicians was to play to enhance one another, provide great dance tempo and produce an overall grand sound. Playing in these conditions brought out the best in the musicians, and this came through when the bands broadcast live. There were no trial runs. It was straight from the shoulder and you could almost feel the adrenaline running till they got settled into their programme. Broadcasting live in those days must have been quite an ordeal when you consider that many players were self taught and some of them could not read music, yet very few mistakes were made. The standard of playing and overall band sound were superb.

In 1956 the Daily Record asked readers to vote for whom they thought to be Scotland's top band. The outcome of this opinion pole was:

1. Jimmy Shand
2. Bobby MacLeod
3. Jim Cameron
4. Ian Powrie
5. Alasdair Downie
6. Jimmy Blair
7. The Wick Scottish Dance Band
8. William Hannah
9. George McAlpine
10. Adam Rennie

This great desire by everyone to dance and listen to Scottish dance music continued into the late fifties, but television came into the home and people's social habits were beginning to change. They were content to watch television and local dance halls and cinemas began to feel the effect of this change with diminishing attendance's. Television shows like the "Kilt is my Delight" and the "White Heather Club" highlighted top bands like Shand, MacLeod and Powrie and were very popular.

The mid sixties saw the beginning of the accordion club scene started by Max Houliston in Dumfries. This provided a great platform for young players to perform in public and still kept a great interest in Scottish dance music by listeners and dancers alike. The following pages show the bands and the year they emerged on to the broadcasting scene from 1945 to 1970.
This information was researched by Farquhar Mathieson of Kirkintilloch and I am most grateful to Farquhar for allowing me to include his work in my book

Year	Band	Origin of Band (where known)
1945	Tim Wright	Edinburgh
	John McArthur	
	Winifred Bird Mathew	Dundee
	Angus Occasionals	Kirriemuir
	Jimmy Shand	Dundee
	Clifford Jordan	Aberdeen
	Harry Ogilvie	Perth
	Tom Johnstone	
	George Davie	
	William Hannah	Falkirk Area
	Scottish Orchestra	
	Glasgow Strathspey & Reel Society	
1946	Kim Murray	Elgin
	Fordyce Strathspey & Reel Society	
	John Day	Grangemouth
	Athole Sextet	
	Kelvingrove Players	Glasgow
	Ernest Wilford	
	Jim Cameron	Kirriemuir, Angus
1947	Scottish Country Dance Players	Edinburgh
	Scottish Mayfair Orchestra	
	John Johnstone	Tranent, East Lothian
1948	The Beechgrove Players	Aberdeen
	David Phin	Dundee
	Elgin Strathspey & Reel Society	Elgin
	The Hawthorn Accordion Band	Blairgowrie, Perthshire
1949	Curly McKay	Aberdeenshire
	Bobby MacLeod	Tobermory, Mull, Argyll
	Angus Fitchet	Dundee
	Ian Powrie	Perthshire
	Stuart Kay	Inverness
	George McAlpine	Condorrat
	Adam Rennie	Coupar Angus, Perthsire

1950   Sandy Anderson   Borders
        Billy McGregor & the Gay Birds   Glasgow
        David Donaldson   Dundee
        Jim Grogan   Dundee
        The Blue Bonnets   Dundee
        Jack Forsyth   Gaurdbridge, Fife
        Annie Shand Scott   Aberdeen
        Hugh McMillan

1951   Archie Alexander   Aberdeen
        Maurice Little   Edinburgh
        The Tayside Dance Band   Dundee
        Nicol Brown
        Jack Cameron
        Cam Robbie   Edinburgh
        Arthur Wallwork
        Andrew Rankine   Menstrie, Clackmannanshire
        Alex Sutherland   Denny, Stirlingshire

1952   Ross's Country Dance Band
        Strathaires   Blairgowrie
        Jimmy Clinkscale   Melrose
        The Gie Gordons   Dundee
        Peter White   Cumnock, Ayrshire
        The Olympians   Fife
        Lindsay Ross   Friockheim, Angus
        Jimmy Taylor   Inverness
        Bob Edward   Dundee
        The Orkney Strathspey & Reel Society   Orkney Isles
        The Wick Scottish Dance Band   Wick, Caithness

1953   Jimmy Blair's Scotia Players   Glasgow
        David Laughton
        Orphir   Orkneys
        Sandy Findlay

1954   Ian Mearns   Elgin
        Alasdair Downie   Appin, Argyll
        Ian Arnott   Perth
        The Mansefield Scottish Dance Quartet   Perth

The Blue Ribbon Scottish Dance Band Crieff
Bert Shorthouse   Kinross

1955   Jim MacLeod   Dunblane
        The Glendaruel Scottish Dance Band   Strathardle, Perthshire
        The Archie Duncan Quartet   Glasgow
        Murray McKillop   Oban, Argyll
        Charles Wall

1957   Jim Crawford   Ladybank, Fife
        The Betty Anderson Quartet   Dundee
        The Highland Country Band   Kellas, Dundee

1958   The Allan Williams Trio   Inverness
        The Heather Scottish Dance Band   Dundee

1959   Jimmy McIntosh   Edinburgh
        The Fair City Scottish Dance Band   Perth
        The Cameron Kerr Scottish Dance Band Dundee
        Syd Chalmers   Forfar
        Isleburgh House Scottish Dance Band Lerwick

1961   Bobby Crowe   Balmullo, Fife

1962   Eric Stewart   Dundee
        Hamish Menzies   Callander
        Ian Holmes   Dumfries

1963   The East Neuk Scottish Dance Band   St. Andrews, Fife
        Ron Gonella   Dundee
        Jim Johnstone   Tranent, East Lothian

1964   Martin Hayes   Blairgowrie
        David Cunningham   Cupar, Fife
        Alisdair Heron   Glasgow
        Johnnie Hastings   Edinburgh
        Alex MacArthur   Elgin
        Willie Simpson   Glenalmond, Perthshire

1965   Jim Baikie   Edinburgh

	Max Houliston	Dumfries
	The Tain Scottish Dance Band	Tain, Ross shire
1966	The Cavendish Dance Band	Edinburgh
	Davie Stewart	Kirriemuir
1967	Jimmy Blue	Perthshire
	Jack Sinclair	Aberdeen
	Fergie McDonald	Argyll
1968	The Glenlomond Dance Band	Kinross
	Hebbie Gray	Keith
	The Hamefarers	Lerwick, Shetland Isles
1969	Fraser McGlynn	Tarbert, Argyll
	Jimmy Lindsay	Perthshire

The Old Masters

The Tim Wright Scottish Dance Band

The Tim Wright band from Edinburgh, broadcast regularly in the early days of Scottish Dance Music on the BBC.

Their style was totally different as they presented music in an orchestrated form. Not quite as exciting as the other bands, nevertheless the band could not be faulted for music or tempo.

The band consisted of five violins, one clarinet, bass, piano and drums. After the death of Tim Wright, Jimmy McIntosh followed on with the same instrument line up. When Jimmy McIntosh died, Andy Bathgate (clarinet) took over and changed the band's name to the Cavendish band. They broadcast a few times when J. Hunter was the producer. Bobby Crowe played accordion with this band from 1968 to 1990.

It was a very busy band and was in great demand for Society Balls etc. North and South of the Border.

The Winifred Bird Mathew Band

Winifred Bird Mathew was a lady who played piano for Scottish country dance classes around Dundee in the forties and early fifties. I'm told she did not particularly like the accordion for Scottish country dancing, preferring the violin.

She broadcast regularly during this period and presented a pleasant, delicate and rhythmical sound, something quite unique.

Her group consisted of:

Winifred Bird Mathew - Piano
Jessie Wilkie, Angus Fitchet - Violin
John White - Bass

When you recognise the players in this group, it can be appreciated how the beautiful sound was obtained.

Jimmy Shand and His Band

What can be written about Jimmy Shand that people don't already know?

He is a virtuoso on the British Chromatic Accordion and undeniably the man who put Scottish dance bands and Scottish dance music where they are today.

When Jimmy made his first broadcast in 1945, he set the whole Scottish dance scene, (Country and Ballroom alike) alive with his band's superb sound; a sound and style that has never altered over the years and certainly no one has managed to produce a band sound quite like it.

His first band was a five piece group. Jimmy on button key accordion, Dave Ireland on violin, George McKelvie on piano accordion, John Knight on piano and Owen McCabe on drums.

The popularity of this band was so great, Jimmy and the boys had to go full time, and what a demanding and star studded career lay ahead for the 'Shand band'.

During the fifties they had a full two year diary of engagements ahead of them at any time. They played Christmas dances at Windsor Castle and Holyrood House and along with television broadcasts in the sixties, they played two Royal Command Performances and six tours to Canada, Australia and America.

Jimmy was awarded the M.B.E. in 1962 and collected three Carl-Alan awards for the most outstanding country dance band leader. He was also Top of the Pops with his recording of the Bluebell Polka.

I was fortunate to have had the pleasure of hearing Jimmy and his band in the Castle Gardens Pavillion in Dunoon in 1950. The line up on that occasion was Jimmy, Syd Chalmers on violin, George McKelvie on piano accordion, Norrie Whitelaw on piano, John White on bass and Owen McCabe on drums.

That was a wonderful night's music, one I shall never forget and I am sure Jimmy Shand will never be forgotten in Scottish dance music circles.

Supporting Players

Excluding those who occasionally sat in, the following is a list of musicians who played in a Shand band:

Second Accordion
George McKelvey, Jimmy Shand Junior, Bert Shorthouse & Jim Johnstone .

Fiddle
Dave Ireland, Angus Fitchet, Jim Ritchie, Syd Chalmers & George Muir.

Piano
Peggy Edwards, Harry Forbes, Johnny Knight, Ab Fields**,**
Norrie Whitelaw, Peter Straughan & Jimmy Scott.

Double Bass
John White, Archie Oliphant, Doug Maxwell, Dave Barclay,
Gordon Lawson, John Strachan & Stan Saunders.

Drums
Owen McCabe, Ian Wilson & Bobby Colgan.

Left to right: George McKelvie (Accordion), Owen McCabe (Drums), Syd Chalmers (Violin), John White (Bass), Jimmy Shand (Accordion), Norrie Whitelaw (Piano)

Photograph by Bert Brown, Dundee

The Jim Cameron Scottish Dance Band

Jim Cameron and his band from Kirriemuir in Angus first broadcast in 1947. They were an immediate hit with the listening and dance public, with their superb swinging sets of tunes for country and old time dancing.

They were a family band with Jim and his brother George on violins, daughter May with nephew Scott on accordions and Willie Ogilvie's subtle use of the trumpet gave this band a unique sound. George Scott on piano and Henry Webster on drums completed the line up. That was the first Jim Cameron band, the second Jim Cameron band comprised:

Jim Cameron - Violin
May Cameron - Piano Accordion
Bill Powrie - British Chromatic Accordion
Dod Michie - Trumpet
Nigel Alexander - Piano
Henry Webster - Drums

I danced to this band in Dunoon and was most impressed by their overall appearance on stage. May in her white evening gown on lead accordion projected this excellent stage presence. They formed a busy and popular band engaged in playing at functions throughout the country, recording and broadcasting regularly up to the mid sixties.

Left to right: Dod Michie (Trumpet), Jim Cameron (Violin), Henry Webster (Drums), May Cameron (Accordion), Bill Powrie (Accordion), Nigel Alexander (Piano)

The John Johnstone Scottish Dance Band

John Johnstone came from Tranent in East Lothian. When he was demobilised from the forces in 1946, he teamed up with his brothers Alex (Atty) and Robb to form his band. The band line up consisted:

John Johnstone - Continental Chromatic Accordion
Alex Johnstone - Continental Chromatic Accordion
Robb Johnstone - Continental Chromatic Accordion
Willie Ramsey - Piano
Willie Turner - Bass
Willie Wilkie - Drums

They auditioned with the BBC and first broadcast in 1947. Their rich, bold sound and great tempo made them very popular with dancers and listeners alike. They played at dances the length and breadth of Britain and finally disbanded in 1965.

I had the pleasure of dancing to this band in Dunoon where it would appear 2 or 3 times a year in the early fifties; something which none of the other big bands at that time could do, thus confirming it's popularity in Dunoon.

A great feature of the band was Willie Ramsay's use of an electric keyboard (claviolin) and Willie Wilkie on vocals during their modern numbers. (During the fifties the top ten numbers were mostly suitable to dance to; quicksteps, modern waltzes and foxtrots).

This was a band leading the field with a superb presentation of music for dancing.

The Hawthorn Accordion Band

This very popular band from Blairgowrie was formed in 1945, by brothers James and Andy Tosh. Their first dance was in Clunie Hall by Blairgowrie in 1945, on "Victory in Europe" night. On platform that night were Jim Tosh and Hamish Millar on accordions, Andy Heron on drums and Andy Tosh on piano.

Several weeks later they were in action again at a "Victory in Japan" night celebration in the same hall.

The band increased in size to seven players, passed a BBC audition in 1947 and broadcast live for the next fifteen years. They were quite unique, with their front line of three accordions and two violins. The line up was as follows:

Jim Tosh - British Chromatic Accordion
Jim Fairweather - Piano Accordion

Both of the above musicians were lead accordionists.

Andy Tosh - Piano Accordion (second accordion)
Jim Howe - Violin
Jimmy Ritchie - Violin
Nigel Alexander - Piano
Tom McDonald - Drums

This was a busy, popular band and I had the pleasure of dancing to them in the early fifties. They were favourites of mine when they broadcast. I was most impressed with their stage appearance and the variety of good music presented in an evening's dancing.

Their popularity took them the length and breadth of the country and they made a few tours in Ireland.

They cut 2 78's, 1 E. P., 2 LP's and 2 cassettes.

This band finally disbanded in 1990.

Left to right: Andy Tosh (2nd Accordion), Jim Howe (Violin), Tom McDonald (Drums), Jim Ritchie (Violin), Jim Tosh (Button Accordion), Nigel Alexander (Piano), Jim Fairweather (Accordion)

The Bobby MacLeod Scottish Dance Band

Bobby MacLeod came from Tobermory on the Isle of Mull in Argyll. He broadcast with his band for the first time in 1949 and was the first West Coast band leader to emerge on the Scottish dance music programmes on the BBC.

I'm sure many will agree with me that Bobby was the man who pointed Scottish dance music in a different direction and gave it the West Coast sound and style, which was completely different from any Scottish dance band sound previously heard.

His use of the second accordion as a rhythm instrument set the pattern most band leaders have adopted ever since to form their bands. Bobby was a piper prior to taking up the accordion and his piping knowledge and skill came through clearly when he included pipe tunes in his selections for Gay Gordons, Barn Dances etc. His perfect timing, phrasing and subtle turn of a note set him worlds apart.

He was undoubtedly the finest exponent of this type of music from the accordion and his great musical skills were aptly displayed in his many fine compositions, tune arrangements and recordings. The MacLeod band had a different style and dance tempos from the more aggressive East coast bands so dominant at that time; and his renderings of Gaelic waltzes were quite unique.

Among his many fine compositions were tunes like *Charlie Hunter, Anne Frazer MacKenzie, Murdo MacKenzie of Torridon, Seamus MacNeill, The Kerrera Polka, Jeans Reel* and *The Lothian Waltz*. He made many recordings. However I think his record "To the Games and Leaving the Games" was way in front of its time and only Bobby could have arranged such fine tunes to portray the atmosphere surrounding a games field. Bobby and his band were very popular and drew large crowds of dancers where ever they were playing. Dunoon was no exception, and I had the pleasure of dancing to Bobby's music in the Castle Gardens Pavilion in the early fifties. The line up at that time was Bobby and Alasdair Downie on accordions, Pibroch MacKenzie on violin, Davy Whitehead on piano, Fen MacDougal on bass and Johnnie Fellows on drums. As a young Scottish dance music enthusiast at that time, Bobby's superb 'violin on top' sound and swinging rhythms really sent my pulse racing. Bobby broadcast regularly with his band in the 1950's. He appeared on television in the "White Heather Club" and toured America and Russia.

Bobby MacLeod, the piper who played an accordion, will always be remembered among Scottish musicians for his great contribution to the Scottish dance music scene.

Bobby MacLeod with his first Marino IV Accordion, later to become the property of Tony Reid, leader of the Glendaruel Scottish Dance Band

Left to right: Fen McDougall (Bass), Hugh Malarkey (2nd Accordion),
Angus McDougall (Drums), Jim Richie (Violin), David Whitehead
(Piano), Bobby MacLeod (Accordion)

Left to right: Derek Auld (Violin), Bobby MacLeod (Accordion),
Willie Low (Bass), Dick MacGill (Drums), David Whitehead (Piano),
Hugh Malarkey (2nd Accordion, was absent because of Influenza)

The Angus Fitchet Scottish Dance Band

Angus Fitchet or the "Dapper Dundonian" as he is often referred to, was a very prominent player during this period of Scottish dance music. His life was spent playing the violin, from the Moorings Cafe in Largs and the silent picture houses, to his retiral from the dance bands in the eighties.

Angus played with Jimmy Shand before forming his own band with which he broadcast regularly from 1948 to 1958. His regular line up was:

Jimmy Steven - Accordion
Angus Fitchet - Violin
Billy Grogan - Second Accordion
John Stuart - Piano
John White - Bass
Bill Black - Drums

An Angus Fitchet broadcast was something to look forward to, superb quality of sound, excellent rhythm and fine sets of tunes.

The highlight for me was always the Scottish Waltzes, in which the violin harmonies were marvellous. A prolific composer, with beautiful tunes like Elizabeth Adair, Princess Margaret's Jig, John Stephen of Chance Inn, Mr Michie and many more. Angus will always be remembered by Scottish dance band musicians.

I had the pleasure of dancing to Angus and his band in Dunoon in the early fifties. The front line on that occasion was Angus and Micky Ainsworth. What a superb combination of fiddle and accordion.

Angus played with most of the Big Bands; Bobby MacLeod, Jimmy Blue, Lindsay Ross, Ian Holmes and Bobby Crowe.

The "Dapper Dundonian" Angus Fitchet

The Ian Powrie Scottish Dance Band

Ian Powrie's first broadcast was at the tender age of twelve, when he played solo violin on the "Children's Hour".

A superb exponent of the violin, he has been involved with his band and as a solo artist in the Scottish dance scene all his life. He played piano accordion in his father's band before forming his own band with his brother Bill (British Chromatic Accordion) in 1947, when they passed an audition with the BBC and broadcast regularly. The first Powrie band was a five-piece group which consisted of:

Ian Powrie - Violin
Bill Powrie - British Chromatic Accordion
Pam Brough - Piano
Bert Smith - Bass
Hugh McIntyre - Drums

The band increased to six piece in 1948 when Jack Ewan on piano accordion joined, followed by Alex MacArthur in 1951. Jimmy Blue on the British Chromatic accordion, took Bill Powrie's seat in 1952 and, around this time Arthur Easson on drums joined the band. This was a fine band. However, I think the greatest Powrie sound emerged when Micky Ainsworth joined the band in 1954, providing that superb front line sound with Ian and Jimmy. Micky's style of playing, coming off the melody line into subtle passages of chords was something special.

During the period from 1956 to 1966 they were one of the busiest bands around in the Scottish dance music scene. They were regularly on television with the "White Heather Club" and the "Kilt is my Delight". Andy Stewart, the popular Scottish singer, engaged the band regularly for his theatre shows and took them on tour; twice to Australia and New Zealand in 1963 and 1966. When the band returned from their second Australian Tour, Ian decided to emigrate to Australia and Jimmy Blue took over.

The final Powrie band of Ian on violin, Jimmy Blue on British Chromatic accordion, Micky Ainsworth on piano accordion, Pam Brough on piano, Dave Barclay on bass and Arthur Easson on drums must go down in the annals of Scottish dance music as one of the greatest Scottish dance band sounds. I'm sure some will go so far as to say, "**The**" greatest.

Right to Left: Jimmy Blue (Button Accordion), Pam Brough (Piano), Ian Powrie (Violin), Bert Smith (Bass), Alex MacArthur (2nd Accordion), Who was the Drummer?

Ian Powrie (Violin), Pam Brough (Piano), Micky Ainsworth (Accordion),
Arthur Easson (Drums), Jimmy Blue (Button Accordion), Dave Barclay (Bass)

The Powrie Band with Harry Carmichael (Piano)

Page 39

The Adam Rennie Scottish Dance Quartet

The Adam Rennie Quartet from Couper-Angus formed a superb one-off Scottish country dance band. Their sound was unique and their style and presentation of Scottish dance music was a pleasure to dancers and listeners alike. The quartet comprised :

Adam Rennie - Violin
Bobby Brown - British Chromatic Accordion
George Robertson - Piano
(Ian MacLeish)
Edd Robb - Bass

They played predominantly for Scottish country dances and Society Balls and were in great demand all over the country.

Adam composed some fine tunes which are included in sets played by the bands of today.

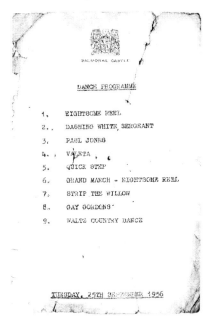

The Famous Quartet.

Left to right: Ian MacLeish (Piano), Edd Robb (Bass), Adam Rennie (Violin), Bobby Brown (Accordion)

Scotch Bachelors' Ball

SHIRE HALL
CHELMSFORD
THURSDAY, 17th JANUARY, 1952

Scotch Bachelors' Ball

IN THE

SHIRE HALL, CHELMSFORD
On Thursday, 17th January, 1952

———— *Adam Rennie* ————
AND
His Broadcasting Scottish Country Dance Quartet

Tickets 25/.   Dancing 8 p.m. - 2 a.m.

Dances		Engagements
1	Waltz	1
2	Quick Step	2
3	Paul Jones	3
4	Highland Schottische	4
5	Veleta	5
6	Circassian Circle	6
7	Quick Step	7
8	Eightsome Reel	8
9	La Rinka	9
10	Petronella	10
11	Waltz	11
		SUPPER
12	Quick Step	12
13	Paul Jones	13
14	Waltz Country Dance	14
15	Medley	15
16	Lancers	16
17	St. Bernard's Waltz	17
18	Dashing White Sergeant	18
19	Fox Trot	19
20	Scottish Reform	20
21	Gay Gordons	21
22	Barn Dance	22
23	Veleta	23
24	Eightsome Reel	24
25	Quick Step	25
26	Duke of Perth, Strip the Willow	26
27	Waltz	27

AULD LANG SYNE

GOD SAVE THE KING

Page 43

The Jim Grogan Band

This Dundee based group was formed in the fifties and broadcast regularly during that period. I had the pleasure of meeting Jim recently, reminiscing over this wonderful period in Scottish dance music.

Jim and his band provided a fine style and sound on their broadcasts. However, they did not play much out of the Perth/ Angus area, as their jobs at that time required them to be on call every day. The line up was:

Jim Grogan - Accordion
Dave Ovenstone - Violin
Bill Robertson - Piano
Angus Fitchet Junior - Drums

This was a band I always enjoyed hearing on the radio. Jim always presented a fine programme of dances with good sets of tunes.

Left to Right: Dave Simpson (Button Accordion), Ken Webster (Bass), Jim Grogan (Piano Accordian), Ron Grogan (Piano)

The Blue Bonnets Scottish Dance Band

A Dundee based band, the Blue Bonnets were formed in 1946 by Jimmy Scott and John Ellis. The first line up was:

Jimmy Scott - Accordion
John Ellis - Violin
John Phillip - Violin
Ron Howie - Drums
Adeline McLay - Piano

Jimmy Scott with his Ranco
Accordion

When Jimmy Scott came back from National Service, he formed the second band, "Jimmy Scott and the Blue Bonnets Scottish Dance Band". The second line up was:

Jimmy Scott - Accordion
Dave Simpson - British Chromatic Accordion
Ron Gonella - Violin
Phylis Harvey - Piano
Tom Conway - Bass
Sandy Fearn - Drums

The Blue Bonnets was a fine band who broadcast regularly till 1962 covering 50 live broadcasts. They were very popular and provided music the length and breadth of the country. I always enjoyed their broadcasts, their sound and tunes arranged for their sets were first class. What a pity they never cut any discs!

Left to right: Dave Simpson (Accordion), Ron Gonella (Violin), Sandy Fearn (Drums), Jimmy Scott (Accordion), Phylis Harvey (Piano)

The Jack Forsyth Scottish Dance Band

"Smiling Jack Forsyth" as he was known, formed his band in 1946. The five piece group passed an audition with the BBC in 1949 and broadcast regularly for many years. Jack was a musical instrument salesman in Dundee. His band with its lively bright sound and tempos, was very popular with both the listening and dancing public.

They made four records on the Beltona label and played at dances throughout the UK.

I had the pleasure of dancing to this band in Strachur hall in the early fifties. On the return journey to Dundee, the band car was involved in an accident in which Jack suffered a broken arm. The band was due to broadcast that evening and at very short notice Jimmy Shand fulfilled the engagement.

The following personnel played in the group:

Jack Forsyth - Accordion
Harry Forbes, Alice Waters - Piano
John Fitchet, Terry Conner, Ron Gonella, Dave Watson - Violin
Archie Oliphant, Dave Barclay - Bass
Tommy Gatherum, Bill Jarvis, Jack Cooper - Drums

Jack Forsyth

Left to right: Dave Watson (Violin), Tommy Gatherum (Drums),
Archie Oliphant (Bass), Jack Forsyth (Accordian), Alice Waters (Piano)

The Tayside Scottish Dance Band

The Tayside Band was a popular band from Dundee, which made its first broadcast in 1951. The line up was as follows:

Marcel Crow - Accordion
Ron Gonella - Violin
Jimmy Muir - Second Accordion
Tam Paton - Piano
Bert Crow - Drums

This was another fine band from an area so rich in excellent musicians. They gave superb presentations on all of their broadcasts.

Left to right: Jim Muir (2nd Accordian), Ron Gonella (Violin), Bert Crow (Drums), Marcel Crow (Accordian), Tom Paton (Piano)

The Andrew Rankine Scottish Dance Band

Andrew Rankine from Menstrie in Clackmannanshire, made his first broadcast with his band on the Scottish dance music programme in 1951. This was a young man who caught the interests of dancers and listeners alike with his bold overall band sound and superb tempos. The first band line up was:

Andrew Rankine - Accordion
Archie Nichol - Violin
Bert Love - Second Accordion
John McIntosh - Piano
Stan Saunders - Bass
Bob Drylie - Drums

This band had a very busy schedule of dances throughout the country, plus regular broadcasts and played together till approximately 1955 when the line up changed to:

Andrew Rankine - Accordion
Bob Christie - Violin
Jack Delaney - Second Accordion
Jimmy Scott - Piano
Stan Saunders - Bass
Andy Hamilton - Drums

The band line up changed again before Andrew moved to Whitley Bay and comprised the following personnel:

Andrew Rankine - Accordion
Ron Kerr - Violin
Ian Holmes - Second Accordion
Robert Campbell - Piano
Tom McTague - Bass
Willie Thom - Drums

Left to right: Andy Hamilton (Drums), Jack Delaney (2nd Accordion), Stan Saunders (Bass), Bobby Findlayson (Violin), Jimmy Scott (Piano), Andrew Rankine (Accordion)

Photograph by kind permission of Jack Delaney

The Gie Gordons Scottish Dance Band

The Gie Gordons Band from Dundee was formed in 1949 and broadcast for the first time in 1952. The line up was as follows:

Ken Stewart - Accordion
Jack Lindsay - Violin
Mick Graham - Piano
Lyall Duncan - Bass
David Glass - Drums

This was a band that always presented a superb programme of Scottish dance music and became very popular with the dancing public throughout the country. Their swinging rhythms and overall fine band sound made them a pleasure to listen to.

Left to right: David Glass (Drums), Jack Lindsay (Violin), Lyall Duncan (Bass), Ken Stewart (Accordion), Mick Graham (Piano)

The Peter White Scottish Dance Band

The Peter White band came from Cumnock in Ayrshire. Peter was head gardener at Ballochmyle hospital and organist at Cumnock Old Parish Church. A very fine musician, he composed dance and church organ music and was held in very high esteem in and around Cumnock.

Ned Rutherford the lead accordionist was Scottish champion in 1947 and second in the British championship in 1948. Peter and Ned played together for over forty years. The Peter White band was very popular throughout Ayrshire and was resident band in Butlins holiday camp for many years. The band first broadcast in 1952 and continued to do so into the mid sixties and recorded three LP's. Jim Littlejohn played second accordion on the three LP's. Peter White's broadcasting band line up was:

Ned Rutherford - Accordion
Rab Simpson - 2nd Accordion
Peter White - Piano
Andrew (Sonny) Scott - Bass
Bill Mackie - Drums

Jim Littlejohn who played
2nd Accordion on Peter
White's 3 LPs

Left to right: Bill Mackie (Drums), Rab Simpson (Accordion),
Ned Rutherford (Lead Accordion), Andrew (Sonny) Scott (Bass),
Peter White (Piano)

The Olympians Scottish Dance Band

This Fife based group was formed in 1950 and first broadcast in 1952. They were very popular and made a big impact on the Scottish dance music scene with their subtle use of the trumpet and lively tight sound.

Not quite the sound of Jim Cameron's band but certainly something different - They started broadcasting as a five piece band with the following line up:

Bobby Crowe - Piano Accordion
Eric Gray - Piano Accordion
Doug Maxwell - Trumpet
David Findlay - Piano
Tommy Robertson - Drums

They made two broadcasts in 1952 minus Eric Gray on accordion. Then in 1953 when Bobby Crowe went on National Service, the band continued with the following line up of musicians:

Martin Hayes - Accordion. Followed by John Huband.
                    Followed by David Cunningham.
Jimmy Yeaman - Violin
Doug Maxwell - Trumpet
David Finlay - Piano
Doug Cargill - Bass
Tommy Robertson - Drums

The band wound up on the death of Doug Maxwell in 1990.

Left to right: Doug Maxwell (Trumpet), Tommy Robertson (Drums), Jimmy Yeaman (Violin), Bobby Crowe (Accordion) David Findlay (Piano), Doug Cargill (Bass)

The Lindsay Ross Scottish Dance Band

Lindsay Ross from Friockheim near Arbroath, formed his first band at the age of fourteen, mainly from members of his own family, playing at local dances in the Angus area. He made his first broadcast on the Scottish dance music programme in 1952 and broadcast regularly for many years. Apart from occasional personnel changes the band line up was as follows:

Lindsay Ross - Accordion
Jim Sturrock - Violin
Marjorie Ross - Piano
Dave Barclay - Bass
Bill Grant - Drums

Angus Cameron (violin) from Kirriemuir played at times with Lindsay and the band.

By the mid fifties with regular broadcasts, the band had a busy schedule of dance engagements with promoters Duncan McKinnon in the "Borders" and Dave Stephen in the "Angus and Mearns" area along with tours of the "Orkneys and Shetlands" and the "Kilt is my Delight" television programmes. Lindsay was a great favourite with the dancing public and musicians because of his fine style; often regarded as having the "velvet touch".

He was an excellent composer and among his many tunes were favourites like *The Family Pride* and *Elegant Esther Gray*.

A Young Lindsay Ross with his Hohner Verdi IV

Left to right: Bill Grant (Drums), Jim Sturrock (Violin), Dave Barclay (Bass), Lindsay Ross (Accordion), Marjorie Ross (Piano)

Left to right: Angus Cameron (Violin), George Sturrock (Drums), Dave Barclay (Bass), Marjorie Ross (Piano), Lindsay Ross (Accordian)

The Wick Scottish Dance Band

The Wick Scottish Dance Band was formed by the very popular and talented violinist Addie Harper. Addie was born at Stirkoke, four miles outside Wick and learned to play the violin during his school years. His teacher was Margaret S. Henderson of Wick, who taught him to play classical violin music. However Addie had no ambitions to be a classical violinist; just a burning desire to play Scottish music in a dance band.

When he was sixteen he gained experience playing with various bands in the Caithness area, and in 1948 he formed the original "Wick Scottish Dance Band". The line up was:

Addie Harper - Violin
Billy Dowler - Accordion
Sandy Meiklejohn - Piano
Jimmy Bain - Drums

This band played together for three years until Billy Dowler decided to return to his native Australia, bringing about the formation of the second Wick Scottish Dance Band. The personnel in this band were:

Addie Harper - Violin
Eann Nicolson - Accordion
David Smith - Piano
Jimmy Bain - Bass
Chris Duncan - Drums

The Wick Scottish Dance Band successfully auditioned and broadcast their first programme of Scottish dance music with the BBC in 1952, broadcasting regularly over the next thirty years.

Their bright lively sound and swinging tempos made them an immediate hit with dancers throughout the country; playing at dances ranging from the Shetland Isles, the Western Isles to as far south as London and the Home Counties. When Addie reminisces over this period with the band, he gives you a feeling of his great satisfaction in having provided music for so many people to enjoy and dance to; even when the journeys were long and often difficult under bad weather conditions.

Apart from playing the violin, Addie also plays the banjo and the Hawaiian guitar. He has composed over one hundred tunes, many of which are played by other bands in their broadcasts. The band had a change of players in the rhythm section in 1964 when Isobel Auld (piano), Hamish Auld (bass) and John Gunn (drums) took the places of Smith, Bain and Duncan.

Addie Harper

Photograph by kind permission of Robert McDonald, Northern Studios, Wick

Who's on the Dance Music Tonight?

B.B.C. Studio, 1952
Left to right: Jimmy Bain (Bass), Chris Duncan (Drums), David Smith (Piano), Addie Harper (Violin), Eann Nicholson (Accordion)

Left to right: Hamish Auld (Bass), Addie Harper (Violin), Isobel Auld (Piano), Eann Nicholson (Accordion), John Gunn (Drums)

Photograph by kind permission of Maurice Harrington of Wick

Page 67

The Ian Mearns Scottish Dance Band

Ian Mearns hailed from Elgin and presented a fine North East lilt and sound with his five piece group.

They broadcast regularly between 1953 to 1957 and played mostly in the North East area, work ties preventing them from playing further afield. Their band work comprised mostly country dances and hotel engagements. The line up was as follows:

Ian Mearns - Violin
Lennox MacLean - Accordion
Rhynas Mitchell - Second Accordion
Bill Armstrong - Piano
George Kessack - Drums

Ian played with the Alex MacArthur band, regrouped in 1977.

Now retired from his job as Town Clerk in Girvan, he still plays with a local band, the Colin McKechnie Scottish Dance Band.

Left to right: Rynas Mitchell (2nd Accordion), George Kessack (Drums), Ian Mearns (Violin), Bill Armstrong (Piano), Lennox MacLean (Accordion)

The Alasdair Downie Scottish Dance Band

Alasdair Downie from Appin in Argyll was a very prominent band leader during the Big Band era from 1945 to 1970.

He started off as a drummer and played for dances in his own locality with Charlie Campbell who played a Hohner Black Dot Double Ray melodeon. Serving his National Service in the Scots Guards from 1946 to 1948 and while based in Aldershot, he managed to buy a second hand piano accordion and taught himself to play.

When he finished his National Service, he formed his first band comprising accordion, violin, piano, drums and trumpet. The band played an audition with the BBC in 1949 but failed to be accepted for broadcasting on that occasion. Alasdair then joined up with Bobby MacLeod and played second accordion with Bobby until 1953. He then formed his own band, played another audition in September 1953 with the BBC and was accepted. The band members were:

Alasdair Downie - Accordion
Calum Skaaras - Violin
David MacKillop - Piano
Maurice Thompson - Bass
Dick McGill - Drums

The band's first broadcast was in 1954 and Jack Fraser took over on violin. What a wonderful sound they presented; a West Coast Sound with plenty of lift and swing. Alasdair and Bobby MacLeod were the only two West Coast bands broadcasting during the fifties when the whole dance scene was alight.

Pibroch McKenzie (violin) and Murray MacKillop (accordion) joined the band in 1955 and this added a greater dimension to the "Downie Sound".

Alasdair's band was always very well presented. I recall dancing to them in Strachur Hall. The band members were in dinner jackets and black bow ties, while Alasdair had a cream dinner jacket and red bow tie. I thought this just added a touch of class to an already very smart outfit.

The Downie band accompanied Calum Kennedy in theatre and as a result of this, Calum recommended the band to Beltona and Decca and they made two records. Derek Auld on violin from Perth joined the band for the first recording session.

Alasdair and his band were very popular throughout the country playing regularly in Glasgow at Highland Balls and functions around the city. The band also played the "Skye Week" regularly during the fifties. One broadcast clearly in my mind was Alasdair's tour of Scotland, taking us around Scotland in dances like *Lasses of Melrose*, *Dundee Reel*, *Trip to Aberdeen*, *Inverness Country Dance*, etc. Something different, certainly something to remember.

The Alasdair Downie band finished broadcasting in 1961.

Left to right: Dick MacGill (Drums), Jack Fraser (Violin & Sax), Maurice Thomson (Bass), Alasdair Downie (Accordion), David MacKillop (Piano)

The Downie Band at Dunvegan Castle during Skye Week

Left to right: Murray MacKillop (Accordion), Billy Ford (Drums),
David MacKillop (Piano), Alasdair Downie (Accordion), Willie Low (Bass)

Alasdair Downie
with his Gaudini Scottish Special Accordion

Page 73

The Ian Arnott Band

Ian Arnott, from Perth, formed his band in the early fifties and broadcast for the first time in 1954.

The line up of this five piece band was -

Ian Arnott - Violin
Frank Thomson - Accordion
Eric Scott - Piano
Bert Smith - Bass
Stan Spiers - Drums

This was a very popular band, always presenting a well balanced programme of Scottish country dance music on their broadcasts. Their popularity took them throughout the country, playing at dances and many high class County Balls of that period.

Bill Hendry replaced Eric Scott on piano and Davie Stewart from Kirriemuir took over the accordian seat from Frank Thomson in 1964. When Ian Arnott emigrated to Australia, Willie Simpson on violin joined the group, and Davie Stewart continued the band in Ian Arnott's name. They finished broadcasting in 1966.

Left to right: Bill Hendry (Piano), Dave Stewart (Accordion),
Bert Smith (Bass), Ian Arnott (Violin), Stan Spiers (Drums)

Photograph by kind permission of Dave Stewart

Page 75

The Bert Shorthouse Quintet

Bert Shorthouse was a very talented musician and accordionist, who first broadcast with his own band in 1954. The line up of this band was:-

Bert Shorthouse - Piano Accordion.
Pam Brough - Piano.
Burt Walker - Euphonium.
Tom Shorthouse - Drums.
Jim Grier - Cornet.

Bert broadcast with this group from 1954 to 1955 before joining Bobby MacLeod's band. During his time playing with Bobby, the MacLeod band was involved in television spots and fulfilled engagements in Moscow, U.S.S.R. He then played with Jimmy Shand for a few years into the mid 1960's, before forming his own "Glenlomond" band, named after an area near Kinross.

This band broadcast during 1968. Bert was a fine all round accordionist.

The Jim MacLeod Scottish Dance Band

Jim MacLeod from Dunblane is one of the longest serving band leaders in the Scottish music scene. From a background of working with a trio on "Children's Hour" in the early fifties, Jim's first broadcast on the BBC "Scottish Dance Music" programme was with the Jim MacLeod Quintet in 1955. The line up consisted of:

Tommy Ford - Accordion
Jim Thomson - Violin
Jim MacLeod - Piano
Chris Duncan - Bass
Alex McMullan - Drums

Jim joined the Reo Stakis organisation at Dunblane Hydro in 1963 in a full time capacity as resident bandleader and promoter, responsible for all events which included television's White Heather Club, Decca recording and up to the present day, filming for Scotdisc.

The band has made countless radio programmes, "Scottish Dance Music", "On Tour", "Radio 2 Ballroom" (where Jim introduced the shows from the stage of Dunblane Hydro), "Friday Night is Music Night" and "Take the Floor". This year they made their 25th visit to Balmoral Castle to play for Her Majesty the Queen at the Gillies Ball. This has always been one of the highlights over the years in the Band's calendar. The Jim MacLeod Band is indeed a show band with a great sound and presentation of Scottish and popular music.

The present line up of the band is Jim on piano, Tommy Ford on accordion, Alex Doig on drums, Jim Clelland on second accordion/keyboard, and John Sinton on bass. Jim wishes to acknowledge the great support he had over the years from the late Jimmy McFarlane who played violin, clarinet, vibes, accordion and piano and Robin Brock who played bass on many of the sessions.

Jim MacLeod and his Band
Left to right: Tommy Ford (Accordion), Jim Clelland (Accordion), Jim MacLeod (Piano), John Sinton (Bass), Alex Doig (Drums)

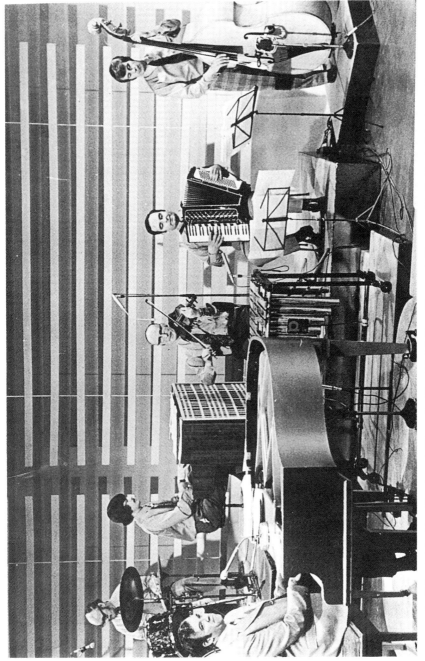

Left to right: Jim MacLeod (Piano), Alex McMullan (Drums), Tommy McCulloch (Keyboard), Jimmy McFarlane (Violin), Tommy Ford (Accordion), Robin Brock (Bass)

The Glendaruel Scottish Dance Band

The "Glendaruel Band" from Bridge of Cally in Perthshire derived their name from their signature tune "The Glendaruel Highlanders".

They were formed in 1952 by a very talented musician and stylish accordionist, Tony Reid. Tony's style was similar to Bobby MacLeod's with whom he was very friendly. The band had the MacLeod swing about it.

They broadcast regularly from 1953 to 1957 and played at dances the length and breadth of the country. They were very popular and I enjoyed a night's dancing to The Glendaruel Band in Dunoon in the early fifties. Dave Stewart from Kirriemuir played second accordion on that occasion, and I shall always remember their lovely rendering of that beautiful Gaelic waltz tune *The Galley of Lorne*.

The regular line up was:

Tony Reid - Accordion
Derek Auld - Violin
Bill Hendry then Eric Stewart - Piano
John Casey - Bass
Watty Crole - Drums

Photograph by kind permission of Louis Flood Photographers, Perth

Left to right: John Casey (Bass), Derek Auld (Violin), Watty Crole (Drums), Tony Reid (Accordion), Bill Hendry (Piano)

The Murray MacKillop Scottish Dance Band

Murray MacKillop from Oban, Argyll, only broadcast under his own name on two occasions. He first broadcast as a quartet in May 1955. The line up was:

Murray MacKillop - Accordion
Colin Bannatyne - Violin
Peter MacKillop - Piano
Duncan Campbell - Bass

This was a broadcast I clearly remember, as I thoroughly enjoyed the superb 'violin on top' sound which Murray and Colin Bannatyne provided by Murray's use of a straight register on his Scandalli accordion, and the lovely tight rhythm from the piano and bass. The second broadcast was in January 1957, this time with the addition of Freddie Nicholson on drums. What a pity Murray didn't broadcast more often!

The Highland Country Band

John Ellis from Wellbank, near Dundee formed the Highland Country Band in 1955. He was previously a founder member of the Blue Bonnets Band along with Jimmy Scott the lead accordionist, and played with them until he went on National Service in 1953. He was based in London during his National Service and enjoyed two years playing with Donnie McBain's Band in that city and around the home counties at high class Highland Balls. The original band personnel was:

John Ellis, John Phillip - Violin
Irene Dear - Accordion
Eileen Simpson - Accordion
Sandy Ford - Drums
Adeline McLay - Piano

The Band auditioned and played its first broadcast for the BBC in 1957 and has broadcast regularly since.

In 1960 Douglas Muir (accordion) joined the band and the front line up of Douglas Muir lead accordion, John Ellis violin and Irene Dear second accordion is still unchanged today. There have been changes in the rhythm section however. The first bass player was Doug Proctor who joined in 1965, followed by Doug Cargill (1970) then Dave Waters in (1990). On piano Catherine Graham joined in 1965, followed by Alice Waters (1970), Sam Cross (1974), Pam Brough (1975), John Gibson (1982) and then Chick Bonar (1986). In 1965 Willie Duthie on drums followed Sandy Ford who was followed by Aly Wilkie (1975), Gordon Smith (1982) and finally George Boath.

The band changed it's name to "John Ellis and the Highland Country Band" in 1968, when it cut it's first LP on the CBS label.

A band with a distinct fine tight sound, it is very popular and has a large following throughout the country.

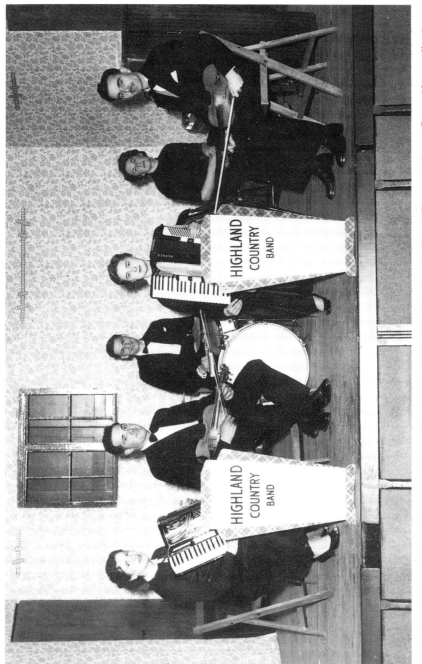

Left to right: Eileen Simpson (Accordion), John Ellis (Violin), Sandy Ford (Drums), Irene Dear (Accordion), Adeline McLay (Piano), John Phillip (Violin)

Left to right: Douglas Muir (Accordion), Chic Bonnar (Piano), John Ellis (Violin), Doug Cargill (Bass), George Boath (Drums), Irene Dear (Accordion)

Page 85

The Allan Williams Trio

This lively trio came from Inverness. Allan on accordion and his brother Lewis on piano, came from Culloden outside Inverness. Drummers George Coutts and Billy Nelson, both from the highland capital, made up the trio on different occasions.

Allan was a self taught player and a superb exponent of the accordion. His broadcasts from 1958 to 1968 were a pleasure to listen to. Great tune arrangements, fine tight rhythm and an overall exciting sound. Allan played on a Hohner Atlantic IV accordian and broadcast a few times on "Down at the Mains" in the children's hour.

He played all over Scotland and the Islands and was the backing group for the "Callum Kennedy Show" on various occasions.

A small group, but a big favourite of many listeners and dancers, myself included.

Allan Williams

Dugald Jenkins and the Heather Scottish Dance Band

The Heather Scottish Dance Band from Dundee, was formed in 1947 and was led by a very talented accordionist Dugald Jenkins. Dugald won the Perth Festival for senior accordionist on two occasions in 1953 and in 1955. He was the first person to be presented with the Jimmy Shand Shield and the presentation was made by the "Maestro" himself. In their early years the band played mainly around the Fife, Perth and Angus area at Scottish country and local dances. They played as a five piece group and broadcast for the first time in 1958. The line up was as follows:

Dugald Jenkins - Accordion
Peem Edwards - Violin
Mac Kinnear - Second Accordion
Johnny Murray - Piano
Jim Thornton - Drums

In the early sixties, Dugald's brother Jim joined the band on double bass and on a few occasions John White deputised. The Heather Band on their broadcasts presented a fine rich sound with superb tempos and their increased popularity took them to play at dances throughout the country.

The band finished playing in 1971 when Dugald emigrated to South Africa.

Left to right: Mac Kinnear (Accordion), Jim Thornton (Drums),
Peem Edwards (Violin), Dugald Jenkins (Accordion), Johnny Murray (Piano)

Dugald Jenkins being presented the Jimmy Shand Shield from the
maestro himself.

Page 89

The Cameron Kerr Scottish Dance Band

The Cameron Kerr Band from Dundee was formed in 1957 by the pianist in the group Angus Cameron Kerr. Angus had great experience in Scottish Country dance music, having played for years as a solo pianist for most of the country dance classes around Dundee.

The band broadcast on the BBC for the first time in 1959 and the line up was as follows:
Tom Clarke - Accordion
Ron Kerr - Violin
Angus Cameron Kerr - Piano
Norrie Gray - Bass
Norrie Ower - Drums
(Ron Gonella took over on violin when Ron Kerr left for National Service)

The Cameron Kerr band always presented an excellent programme of dance music in their broadcasts. Superb sets of tunes and dance tempos along with a grand overall sound, made them great favourites over their many years of broadcasting.

The Cameron Kerr SCD Band

Left to right: Angus Cameron Kerr (Piano), Tom Clark (Accordion), Norrie Gray (Bass), Norrie Ower (Drums), Ron Gonella (Violin)

Page 91

Three of the Best, "Having a Tune"

Left to right: Bobby MacLeod, Angus Fitchett and Jimmy Shand

A Gathering of Celebrities at Dunblane

Left to right, back row: Jack Cooper, Jimmy Shand, Angus Fitchett, Jimmy Blue, Andrew Rankin,
Andy Stewart, George Stirrat, Bobby Crowe, Dave Barclay.
Left to right, front row: Ron Gonella, Stan Saunders, Jimmy Yeaman, Jack Delaney

Young Masters

The Bobby Crowe Scottish Dance Band

Bobby Crowe from Balmullo in Fife has been involved in the Scottish dance band scene since the early fifties. He was an original member of the Olympians dance band before forming his own dance band in 1955. A superb exponent of the piano accordion, Bobby's band had its own style and top quality sound. He auditioned with the BBC in September 1960. His first broadcast was on the 4th December 1961 after which he broadcast regularly for many years. Bobby also played with the Cavendish band in London. The line up of his original band was:

Bobby Crowe - Piano Accordion
Bobby Crease - Violin
Mike Hamilton - Piano
Wiam Skinner - Bass
Collin Lander - Drums

Bobby's band was very popular and in great demand in Scottish country dance circles north and south of the border. He cut eleven records for the "Royal Scottish Country Dance Society" and three commercial discs with his band. Latterly Bobby's band line up was:

Bobby Crowe - Accordion
Edward Galley - Second Accordion
Ron Kerr - Violin
James Lindsay - Piano
Dave Barclay - Bass
Malcolm Ross - Drums

The Bobby Crowe band had a truly great sound and is greatly missed from the broadcasting and Scottish dance scene.

Left to right: Collin Lander (Drums), Bobby Crease (Violin), Wiam Skinner (Bass), Mike Hamilton (Piano), Bobby Crowe (Accordion)

The Hamish Menzies Scottish Dance Band

Hamish Menzies from Callander played with the local "Glengarry Band", before forming his own group in 1960. He broadcast for the first time with the BBC in 1961; the line up of the band being:

Jack Delaney - Piano Accordion
Hamish Menzies - Violin
Dochie McCallum - British Chromatic Accordion
Jimmy Scott - Piano
Stan Saunders - Bass
Bert Leishman - Drums

1962 brought about a complete change in the rhythm section with Walter Sinton (piano), John Buchanan (bass) and Gus Millar (drums) joining the band.

They were a very popular band wherever they played and broadcast regularly till they disbanded in 1972.

Left to right: Dochie McCallum (Button Accordion), Bert Leishman (Drums), John Buchannan (Bass), Hamish Menzies (Violin), Walter Sinton (Piano), Jack Delaney (Piano Accordion)

Ian Holmes
Scottish Dance Band

Ian Holmes is from Dumfries and took up playing the accordion in his teens. He played in several local bands and had the opportunity of sitting in with some of the big bands including Shand, MacLeod and Powrie in the early Fifties when they were playing around the Dumfries area. Ian joined the Andrew Rankine band in 1960 and played with Andrew up to 1962, broadcasting regularly over that period. He then formed his own band, making its first broadcast that same year. The band line up was:

Ian Holmes - Piano Accordion
Kenny Wilson - Violin
Davy Whitehead - Piano
Stan Saunders - Bass
Bert Leishman - Drums

This was a very successful debut broadcast and Ian has made over one hundred broadcasts throughout the years. Jimmy Shand called in to the Edinburgh studio that evening to wish him success, a gesture Ian appreciated very much.

Ian has been a great admirer of Bobby MacLeod as an accordionist and band leader and this has certainly influenced the style and sound of his own band. I am sure few would disagree when I say it's difficult to differentiate between the old master and the young master when pipe music is played. Ian's skill in playing pipe marches is quite exceptional. During the late sixties there were three personnel changes in his band;

Bill Henry on piano, Bobby McNeillie on second accordion and Gordon Young on drums joined the group.

A prolific composer, Ian has penned some fine tunes in both Scottish and Continental music. Some of my favourite compositions are *Hills of Tynron, Queen of the South Polka, Mrs Margaret Holmes' Strathspey* and *Thoughts of Bobby MacLeod.* Among his many Continental compositions are *Memories of Norway, Borjes Polka* and *Echo's From Adelbonen.*

Ian's contribution to the dance band and accordion scene over the years has been outstanding.

Left to right: Stan Saunders (Bass), Bobby McNeillie (2nd Accordion), Kenny Wilson (Violin), Bill Henry (Piano), Ian Holmes (Accordion), Gordon Young (Drums)

Ian with his 5 row Hohner Morino Continental Chromatic Accordion

Page 103

The Jim Johnstone Scottish Dance Band

Jim Johnstone from Tranent in East Lothian is one of the most experienced accordionists and band leaders around today. He first broadcast solo on the 'Children's Hour' in 1950 and has been to the forefront of Scottish dance music over the years. A nephew of John Johnstone, Jim broadcast with his uncle's band in their latter years. He played with Andrew Rankine before broadcasting with his own band from 1963 to 1966. On deciding to go full time he played with Jimmy Shand's band and the Jimmy Blue band. Jim reformed his own band in 1968 and has been broadcasting regularly ever since. The original line up was:

Jim Johnstone - Piano Accordion
Alan Johnstone - Violin
Dave Flockhart - Piano
Robin Brock - Bass
Bobby Colgan - Drums

The Jim Johnstone Band has a grand sound, great tempos and is a delight to both dancer and listener alike. There have been various personnel changes in the band over the years but Jim's distinct band sound and style have never altered. Among his many fine compositions are *Billy Thom's Reel, Drumloist* and *Waltz for Tracy*; tunes which are regularly played by other bands in their broadcasts. Jim Johnstone and his band are very popular and have a great following throughout the country.

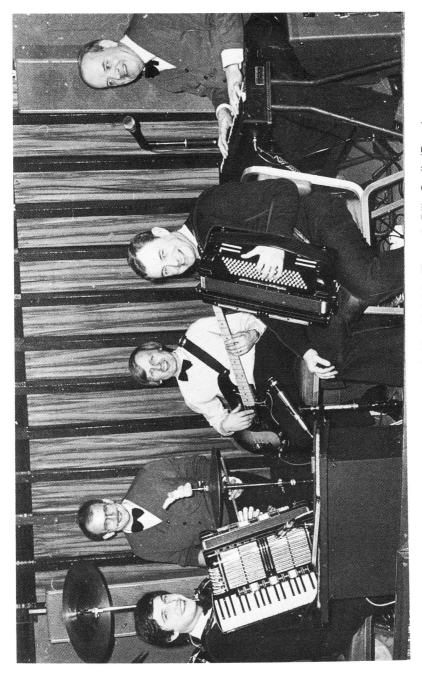

Left to right: Neil Barron (2nd Accordion), Max Ketchin (Drums), Billy Craib (Bass), Jim Johnstone (Accordion), Bobby Brown (Piano)

Page 105

The Alex MacArthur Scottish Dance Band

Alex MacArthur, or the "General" as he was known in band circles, broadcast with his own band from 1963 to 1970. Formerly with the Arthur McLeod Trio and Ian Powrie Band, Alex played the piano accordion with tremendous rhythm and style. His domino registered Morino IV accordian of early fifties vintage had a unique powerful sound and Alex used it to it's great advantage. His band broadcast regularly out of Aberdeen and Inverness and worked throughout Scotland. A very popular band and Alex a most friendly character. The personnel of his band was as follows:

Alex MacArthur - Accordion
Rhynas Mitchell - Second Accordion
Ian Mearns - Violin
Ann Grant - Piano
Sandy Fraser - Bass
Monty Smillie - Also Bass
Billy Nelson - Drums
Alasdair Stewart - Drums

Alex formed a second band in 1977 comprising:

Alex MacArthur - Accordion
Dave Stewart, Jack Delaney and
        John Douglas - Second Accordion
Ian Mearns - Violin
Ian Wilson - Piano
Billy Craib - Bass
Billy Grant - Drums

The Original Alex MacArthur Broadcasting Band
Left to right: Alex MacArthur (Accordion), Ann Grant (Piano), Alastair Stewart (Drums),
Rhynas Mitchell (2nd Accordion), Sandy Fraser (Bass)

The David Cunningham Trio

David Cunningham first broadcast on "Children's Hour" in 1956, followed by regular appearances on programmes such as BBC Radio's for "Young Entertainment", "Come Thursday" and "Woman's Hour", being accompanied by Harry Carmichael, Jill Stewart and other BBC 'Staff' accompanists of the time.

He turned full time professional in 1960 appearing in variety theatres around the country along with artistes as diverse as Donald Peers (By a Babbling Brook), Johnny Beattie, Danny Steet and Glen Daly (Mr Glasgow).

David Joined the Olympians Dance Band in 1961. He then formed the David Cunningham Trio comprising David on Accordion, David Findlay on Piano and Doug Cargill on Bass to fulfil an engagement on a BBC "Come Thursday" programme playing French and German music.

The David Cunningham Trio broadcast on the 'Scottish Dance Music' programme for the first time in 1964 and broadcast regularly into the late seventies when other commitments forced David to give up the trio and stop broadcasting. They were a small group with a big bold sound and always presented fine selections of tunes in their broadcasts. Great favourites of mine and a band I always looked forward to hearing.

Left to right: David Cunningham (Accordion), Doug Cargill (Bass),
David Findlay (Piano)

Page 109

The Max Houliston Scottish Dance Band

Max Houliston from Dumfries, younger brother of the already famous Scottish International football player Billy Houliston, started playing the accordion in the early fifties and formed his first band in 1959. They played at dances mainly in South West Scotland and the Borders in their early years before auditioning with the BBC in 1965, and broadcasting later that year. The band line up was:

Max Houliston - Piano Accordion
Kenny Wilson - Violin
Ian Austin - Piano
Gordon Young - Bass
Steve Redpath - Drums

This band broadcast regularly for the next eight years and was very popular. They had lovely rhythms, a beautiful relaxed style and rich sound. Their workload now covered the length and breadth of the country, touring with the "David Webster Scottish Show" throughout England and three tours to Canada. They had regular early evening spots on Border Television which were very popular during the seventies. It was nice to hear Max broadcast again recently after a long layoff. The old Houliston sound and style are still there.

Left to right: Gordon Young (Bass), Max Houliston (Accordion), Ian Austin (Piano), Steve Redpath (Drums), Kenny Wilson (Violin)

Max Houliston with his trusty Morino V

The Jimmy Blue Scottish Dance Band

When Ian Powrie emigrated to Australia in 1966, Jimmy Blue, who had been the lead accordionist for many years, took over the Powrie Band and renamed it the Jimmy Blue Scottish Dance Band. Jimmy's influence on the Powrie Band's sound had been such as to render that of the Jimmy Blue Band almost identical. Jimmy enlisted the services of Ron Kerr on violin to replace Ian and broadcast under his own name for the first time in 1967.

The next ten years saw Jimmy and his band involved in a much broader field with their music. Regular broadcasting, television spots (Scotch Corner), recording and theatre work along with tours of America, Canada, Rhodesia and South Africa kept them on a very busy schedule. They were also involved in the film "Country Dance", starring Peter O'Toole and Susannah York filmed on location in Co. Wicklow in Ireland in 1969.

Among other fine musicians who played in the Jimmy Blue Band were Angus Fitchet (violin), Jim Johnstone, Dave Stewart, Jim Cassidy (accordion) and Bobby Colgan (drums).

Left to right: Pam Brough (Piano), Dave Barclay (Bass), Jim Johnstone (2nd Accordion), Bobby Colgan (Drums), Jimmy Blue (Accordion)

Jimmy Blue
Photograph by kind permission of Bill Wright , Kirkcaldy

The Hamefarers Scottish Dance Band

The original Hamefarers Dance Band from Shetland was formed after a visit to those Northern Isles from the Ian Powrie band in 1965. The line up was as follows:

Ronnie Cooper - Accordion
Willie Hunter - Violin
Jim Halcrow - Accordion
Eric Cooper - Piano
Willie Johnson - Bass
Drew Robertson - Drums

They were not another Powrie Band, but something quite exceptional with their own style of playing Shetland music. Their overall musicianship, tempos and marvellous band sound made them quite unique. The front line members of the band were all fine composers, penning beautiful tunes like *Doreen's Waltz* (Jim Halcrow), *Leaving Lerwick Harbour* (Willie Hunter), *St. Ninians Isle* (Ronnie Cooper) and many more. They broadcast for the first time in 1967 and were very popular on their tours of accordion clubs throughout Scotland.

Left to right: Jim Halcrow (Accordion), Drew Robertson (Drums), Willie Hunter (Violin), Willie Johnson (Bass), Ronnie Cooper (Accordion), Eric Cooper (Piano)

The Fraser McGlynn Scottish Dance Band

Fraser McGlynn from Tarbert in Argyll formed his first band, a six piece group in 1955. The line up of the band was:-

Fraser McGlynn - Three row British chromatic accordion.
Davey Scott - Violin.
Duncan McLean - Piano Accordion.
Jimmy Flaherty - Piano.
Norman Smith - Bass.
Jackie McLeod - Drums.

This band played predominantly in Mid Argyll and Kintyre until Fraser successfully auditioned with the BBC and started broadcasting in the late 1960's. The band was now a five piece group and their music took them throughout the country playing at dances and accordion clubs. The line up was as follows:-

Fraser McGlynn - Three row British chromatic accordion.
Davey Scott - Violin.
Duncan McKay - Piano.
Sandy Black - Bass.
Willie Robertson - Drums.

The Fraser McGlynn band was very popular, having a very distinct West Coast style and always presented a superb programme of dance music in their broadcasts. A great pleasure to listen to.

Left to right: Willie Robertson (Drums), Sandy Black (Bass), Duncan McKay (Piano), Davey Scott (Violin), Fraser McGlynn (Accordion)

The Jimmy Lindsay Scottish Dance Band

Jimmy Lindsay from Glenalmond in Perthshire, formed his band in 1967 and first broadcast with the BBC in 1969. The line up of his band was as follows:

Jimmy Lindsay - British Chromatic Accordion
Jack Lindsay - Violin
Ian Anderson - Second Accordion
Joan Blue - Piano
Ron Dunn - Bass
Bob Doig - Drums

Jimmy's band had a fine rich sound, superb dance tempos and soon became very popular particularly with Scottish country dance clubs throughout Scotland and England in the 1970's.

He cut a disc for the "Royal Scottish Country Dance Society" in 1977 for book 28 and his band played for the Royal Family Jubilee celebrations in Dundee City Square. Over the years, various other musicians have played in the Jimmy Lindsay Band. Bill Hendry, Ray Milburn and Pam Brough (piano), Dave Stewart (second accordion), Stan Peacock and Ally Wilkie (drums) and Bill Morgan (bass).

Jimmy Lindsay

The Supporting Musicians

Having highlighted many of the prominent bands and their leaders, it is only right to give an appreciation to the supporting musicians, as without their skills and musicianship the great bands of that era would not have had their great public appeal.

The violin was played in most of the bands at that time, giving that superb 'violin on top' sound. The accordions of course were not tuned as widely as they are today, thus blending beautifully with the violin. Needless to say there were many fine exponents of the violin.

The skillful second accordionists contributed much to the bands. No matter whether they were playing the melody line, or melody line combined with emphasised chord passages or simply chords, they assuredly enlarged the whole band sound.

The rhythm section of piano, bass and drums is the real backbone to a good band and there was an abundance of good musicians on these instruments throughout the broadcasting bands of that period.

Many of the well known instrumentalists participating during that time are listed in the following pages.

Violinists

Who's on the Dance Music Tonight?

Violinist	Band
Derek Auld.	The Mansfield Scottish Dance Quartet, Glendaruel Band, Bobby MacLeod & Alasdair Downie.
Colin Bannatyne.	Murray MacKillop.
Angus Cameron.	Lindsay Ross.
Syd Chalmers.	Jimmy Shand.
Bob Christie.	Andrew Rankine, Alasdair Downie, Jim Johnstone & Ian Holmes.
Terry Conner.	Jack Forsyth, Betty Anderson & Bobby Crowe.
Bobby Crease.	Bobby Crowe.
Peem Edwards.	The Heather Broadcasting Band.
John Ellis.	The Highland Country Band & the Blue Bonnets.
Bobby Findlayson.	Andrew Rankine.
Angus Fitchet	Jimmy Shand, Winifred Bird Mathew, Bobby MacLeod, Lindsay Ross, Jimmy Blue, Ian Holmes and Bobby Crowe
John Fitchet	Jack Forsyth.
Jack Fraser.	Alasdair Downie.
Ron Gonella.	Cameron Kerr Band, Jack Forsyth, the Blue Bonnets & the Tayside Scottish Dance Band.
Addie Harper.	Wick Scottish Dance Band.
Jim Howe.	Hawthorn Accordion Band.
Willie Hunter.	The Hamefarers.
Dave Ireland	Jimmy Shand.
Alan Johnstone	Jim Johnstone.
Ron Kerr.	Cameron Kerr Band, Bobby Crowe, Jim Johnstone, Jimmy Blue & Andrew Rankine.
Jack Lindsay.	The Gie Gordons, Bobby Crowe & Jimmy Lindsay.
Jimmy McFarlane.	Jim MacLeod.
Alex "Pibroch" MacKenzie.	Bobby MacLeod. Alisdair Downie
George Muir	Jimmy Shand.
Archie Nichol	Andrew Rankine
Dave Ovenstone.	Jim Grogan.
John Phillip.	The Highland Country Band & the Blue Bonnets.
Jimmy Ritchie.	Bobby MacLeod, Jimmy Shand & the Hawthorn Accordion Band.
Willie Simpson	Ian Arnott.
Bobby Sinclair	Andrew Rankine.
Calum Skaaras	Alisdair Downie.
David Scott.	Fraser McGlynn.
Jim Sturrock.	Jack Forsyth & Lindsay Ross.

Jim Thomson
Dave Watson.
Jessie Wilkie
Kenny Wilson.
Jimmy Yeaman.

Jim MacLeod
Jack Forsyth.
Winifred Bird Mathew.
Ian Holmes & Max Houliston.
Olympians Dance Band.

Alex Pibroch McKenzie (Violin)

Pibroch McKenzie came from Inverness and was very much involved in the Scottish Dance Band Scene of the forties and fifties. He played with Bobby MacLeod's band for a few years, then with Alasdair Downie. What a grand player Pibroch was with Bobby and Alasdair. His style of playing suited both band leaders down to a tee. Pibroch gave both bands their superb 'violin on top' sound and he could bring in shades of 'Grappelli' when playing quicksteps and foxtrots.

Syd Chalmers (Violin)

Syd Chalmers from Forfar, was another of Scotland's top violinists in the period covered by this book. He played with Jimmy Shand during the heyday of Jimmy's band. Syd was also a very fine soloist.

Jimmy Ritchie

Jimmy Ritchie, the Fiddler O' Glenshee, had a star studded career during the halcyon days of Scottish dance music. He played in three of the top bands during that period. The Hawthorn Accordion Band, Bobby MacLeod's band and Jimmy Shand's band.

Jimmy is a fine violinist; both solo and as a band player. Among his many compositions are popular tunes like *Helen Black of Inveran, Jimmy Shand MBE, Airlie Bobbies* and *C.M. Hall.* He still plays occasionally with Robert MacLeod and Jimmy Shand Junior.

Ron Gonella (Violin)

Ron Gonella

Ron Gonella was a very active musician during the halcyon days of Scottish dance music. He played with Jack Forsyth, the Tayside Band, the Blue Bonnets, the Cameron Kerr Band and Lindsay Ross. Ron was one of Scotland's top violinists and a very popular and successful solo artist. The haunting sound of his violin and his expression when playing slow airs were something to treasure.

Bob Christie (Violin)

Bob Christie from Stirling is held in very high regard in the Scottish dance music scene as both a solo violinist and a band musician. He played as a soloist in the programme "Scottish Fiddle Music" in the fifties and has played with prominent bands like Andrew Rankine, Alasdair Downie, Jim Johnstone and many more. Bob is a player who enhances the front line of any band.

Derek Auld (Violin)

Derek Auld from Perth, first broadcast with the Mansfield Scottish Dance Quartet in 1954 on their sole broadcast. He then broadcast with the Glendaruel Band. His bold style of playing along with Tony Reid on accordion, produced a sound quite similar to that of Bobby MacLeod's band. He played with Bobby Macleod from 1957 to 1958, then played with Bill Powrie from 1959 to 1961. Derek played violin for Alasdair Downie when he cut his first LP.

Ron Kerr (Violin)

Ron Kerr from Monifieth, is one of the most experienced violin players on the Scottish dance music scene. He made his first broadcast solo on the BBC in the "Children's Hour" when he was eleven years old and is still broadcasting with several major bands.

A superb exponent of the violin, Ron's style adds lustre to any band of which he is a member. He played with Lindsay Ross, Jim Grogan, Jim Johnstone, Andrew Rankine, Jimmy Blue and Bobby Crowe.

Accordionists

Accordionist	Band
Mickey Ainsworth.	Angus Fitchet & Ian Powrie.
Ian Anderson.	Jimmy Lindsay.
Jimmy Blue.	Ian Powrie.
Bobby Brown	Adam Rennie.
Jim Cassidy	Jimmy Blue
May Cameron.	Jim Cameron.
Scott Cameron.	Jim Cameron.
Tom Clark.	Cameron Kerr Scottish Dance Band.
Jim Clelland	Jim MacLeod
Ronnie Cooper.	The Hamefarers.
Marcel Crow.	The Tayside Scottish Dance Band.
Bobby Crowe.	Olympians Scottish Dance Band.
David Cunningham	Olympians Scottish Dance Band
Irene Dear.	The Highland Country Band.
Jack Delaney.	Andrew Rankine & Hamish Menzies.
John Douglas.	Max Houliston.
Billy Dowler	Wick Scottish Dance Band
Archie Duncan.	Jimmy Blair's Scotia Players & BBC Orchestra.
Jack Ewan	Ian Powrie
Jim Fairweather.	Hawthorn Accordion Band.
Tommy Ford.	Jim MacLeod.
Edward Galley	Bobby Crowe
Eric Gray.	Olympians Scottish Dance Band.
Bill Grogan.	Angus Fitchet.
Jim Halcrow.	The Hamefarers.
Martin Hayes.	Olympians Scottish Dance Band.
John Huband	Olympians Scottish Dance Band
Alistair Hunter	Hebbie Gray.
Dugald Jenkins.	The Heather Scottish Dance Band.
Alex Johnstone	John Johnstone
Jim Johnstone	Jimmy Shand, John Johnstone and Jimmy Blue
Rob Johnstone	John Johnstone
Mac Kinnear.	The Heather Scottish Dance Band.
Jim Littlejohn	Peter White
Bert Love	Andrew Rankine
Alex MacArthur	Ian Powrie
Dochie MacCallum	Hamish Menzies
George McKelvie.	Jimmy Shand.
Murray MacKillop	Alasdair Downie
Duncan McLean	Fraser McGlynn
Lennox McLean.	Ian Mearns.
Bobby McNeillie.	Ian Holmes.
Hugh Malarkey.	Bobby MacLeod & Ian Holmes.
Rhynas Mitchell	Alex MacArthur, Ian Mearns

Douglas Muir	Highland Country Band
Jimmy Muir.	Tayside Scottish Dance Band.
Eann Nicholson.	Wick Scottish Dance Band.
Ian Nicholson.	Wick Scottish Dance Band.
Bill Powrie.	Ian Powrie & Jim Cameron.
Tony Reid.	Glendaruel.
Ned Rutherford	Peter White.
Jimmy Shand Jnr	Jimmy Shand
Bert Shorthouse.	Bobby MacLeod & Jimmy Shand.
Dave Simpson.	Blue Bonnets.
Eileen Simpson.	The Highland Country Band.
Rab Simpson	Peter White
Jimmy Stephen.	Angus Fitchet.
Dave Stewart.	Ian Arnott, Glendaruel, Jimmy Blue & Jimmy Lindsay.
Ken Stewart	Gie Gordons
Alex Sutherland	George McAlpine.
Frank Thomson.	Ian Arnott.
Andy Tosh.	Hawthorn Accordion Band.
Jim Tosh.	Hawthorn Accordion Band.
George Watson.	The Mansfield Scottish Dance Quartet.

Jimmy Blue and Micky Ainsworth

Jimmy Blue and Micky Ainsworth first met at a two band dance in Auchterarder in 1949. Jimmy was playing in Hamish McLaren's Scottish Dance Band and Micky in the modern band "The Skyliners"

Jimmy's style of playing Scottish music on the three row British Chromatic accordion caught Micky's imagination and a partnership was immediately formed. So successful was the partnership, they almost became a household name among accordion enthusiasts, with duets on many radio programmes and records, some of which are now collector's items.

Jimmy Blue was born in Newton Mearns near Glasgow. He spent most of his youth in Clynder, Dunbartonshire from where he travelled to see and hear the legendary Will Starr play in Helensburgh. From that moment all he dreamt of was playing the "button box"!

To obtain tuition would have meant going to Glasgow which was not possible, so Jimmy sent for the "Mathis Method" and persevered alone not only to learn to play the accordion, but also to read music.

Jimmy's family decided in 1949 to move to Perthshire and what could be a better move for such a talented young accordion player? He was now right in among the top bands of that area and what a musical career lay ahead with the Powrie band and eventually his own band.

Micky Ainsworth came from Leeds to reside in Auchterarder when he was eight years old. He was always keen on music and taught himself to read music and play the accordion. Not until he met Jimmy Blue did he develop an interest in Scottish dance music, having previously been involved in modern and swing music with the "Skyliners".

Micky joined the Angus Fitchet band in the early fifties, taking over from Jimmy Stevens. He then teamed up with Jimmy Blue in the legendary Ian Powrie band of the fifties and sixties. In the late sixties, Micky was Hohner's representative in Scotland, Ireland and the North of England, but after surviving a serious car crash in 1972, he left Hohner and returned to teaching and freelance accordion and piano playing.

What a fine duo Jimmy Blue and Micky Ainsworth was. Superb exponents of their accordions and great ambassadors of Scottish dance music.

It has been my pleasure to have met both of them.

Dave Stewart (Accordion)

Dave Stewart comes from Kirriemuir in Angus and has been involved in the Scottish dance music scene all of his working life. A superb accordionist and session musician, his experience in this field is second to none. He played with Ian Arnott, the Glendaruel Band, the great Jimmy Blue band of the seventies, broadcast with his own band and was involved in recording sessions with Lindsay Ross and Alex MacArthur.

Jack Delaney (Accordion)

Another fine musician from Alloa with over 40 years experience, Jack played second accordion with Andrew Rankine and lead accordion with the Hamish Menzies band from Callander. Jack broadcast with his own band from 1982 to 1987 and was involved in recording sessions with the Alex MacArthur band.

Tommy Ford (Accordion)

Tommy Ford from Stirling, is quite unique among Scottish dance band accordionists in as much that he has played with one band only; that of Jim MacLeod's. Jim and Tommy have played together for over forty years and his experience in the show band business is second to none. Tommy has always played a Ranco accordion and contributes greatly to the distinctive sound of the Jim MacLeod Band. A superb accordionist, Tommy is very popular in the band and as a solo player at accordion clubs.

Pianists

Who's on the Dance Music Tonight?

Pianist	Band
Nigel Alexander.	Hawthorn Accordion Band & Jim Cameron.
Bill Armstrong.	Ian Mearns Scottish Dance Band.
Isobel Auld	The Wick Scottish Dance Band
Ian Austin.	Max Houliston.
Marjorie Barclay (Nee Ross).	Lindsay Ross & Jim Cameron.
Joan Blue.	The Mansfield Scottish Dance Quartet & Jimmy Lindsay.
Chick Bonar	Highland Country Band
Pam Brough.	Ian Powrie & Bert Shorthouse.
Bobby Brown	Jim Johnstone
Robert Campbell.	Andrew Rankine.
Gordon Clark.	Ian Powrie.
Eric Cooper.	The Hamefarers.
Sam Cross	Highland Country Band
Peggy Edwards	Jimmy Shand
Ab Fields	Jimmy Shand
David Findlay.	Olympians Scottish Dance Band.
Jimmy Flaherty	Fraser McGlynn
Dave Flockhart	Jim Johnstone
Harry Forbes.	Jack Forsyth, Jimmy Shand & Angus Fitchet.
John Gibson	Highland Country Band
Mick Graham	Gie Gordons Scottish Dance Band
Ann Grant.	Alex MacArthur.
Mike Hamilton.	Bobby Crowe.
Phylis Harvey.	Blue Bonnets & Hawthorn Accordion Band.
Bill Hendry.	Ian Arnott, Glendaruel Scottish Dance Band, Bobby Crowe & Jimmy Lindsay.
Bill Henry.	Ian Holmes & Jim Johnstone.
Angus Cameron Kerr.	Cameron Kerr Scottish Dance Band.
James Lindsay	Bobby Crowe
Duncan McKay.	Fraser McGlynn.
David MacKillop.	Alasdair Downie.
Peter MacKillop.	Murray MacKillop.
John McIntosh.	Andrew Rankine.
Adeline McLay.	Highland Country Band & Blue Bonnets.
Ian McLeish	Adam Rennie
Sandy Meiklejohn	Wick Scottish Dance Band
Ray Milburn	Jimmy Lindsay.
Johnny Murray.	The Heather Scottish Dance Band.
Tom Paton.	Tayside Scottish Dance Band.
Willie Ramsay.	John Johnstone.
Bill Robertson.	Jim Grogan.
Geroge Robertson.	Adam Rennie.
Eric Scott.	Ian Arnott.
Jimmy Scott.	Andrew Rankine, Jimmy Shand & Ian Holmes.

Walter Sinton
David Smith.
Eric Stewart.
Peter Straughan
John Stuart.
Alice Waters.

Lewis Williams.
David Whitehead.
Norman Whitelaw.
Ian Wilson

Ian Menzies.
Wick Scottish Dance Band.
Glenadaruel Scottish Dance Band.
Jimmy Shand
Angus Fitchet.
Jack Forsyth, Lindsay Ross & the
Highland Country Band.
Allan Williams Trio.
Bobby MacLeod & Ian Holmes.
Jimmy Shand.
Alex MacArthur

Pianists

As with drummers, it is difficult to find solo photographs of pianists. I have been fortunate to obtain one of the doyen of the business, Pam Brough. Pam was almost a household name as were the other members of the Powrie Band in which she played throughout it's peak years.

Bass Players

Bass Player	Band
Hamish Auld	Wick Scottish Dance Band
Jimmy Bain.	Wick Scottish Dance Band.
Dave Barclay.	Jack Forsyth, Lindsay Ross, Ian Powrie, Jimmy Shand, Jimmy Blue & Bobby Crowe.
Jimmy "Dinger" Bell.	Bobby MacLeod & Alasdair Downie.
Sandy Black.	Fraser McGlynn.
Robin Brock	Jim MacLeod & Jim Johnstone.
John Buchanan.	Hamish Menzies.
Duncan Campbell.	Murray MacKillop.
John Casey.	Glendaruel Scottish Dance Band.
Doug Cargill.	Olympian Scottish Dance Band, Highland Country Band & David Cunningham Trio
Tom Conway.	Blue Bonnets.
Billy Craib.	Jim Johnstone & Alex MacArthur
Christie Duncan.	Jim MacLeod.
Lyall Duncan.	Gie Gordons Scottish Dance Band.
Ron Dunn.	Jimmy Lindsay.
Sandy Fraser.	Alex MacArthur.
Norrie Gray.	Cameron Kerr Scottish Dance Band.
Jim Jenkins.	The Heather Scottish Dance Band.
Willie Johnson.	The Hamefarers.
Gordon Lawson	Jimmy Shand
Willie Low.	Bobby MacLeod.
Fen McDougal.	Bobby MacLeod.
Tom McTague.	Andrew Rankine, Ian Holmes & Bobby MacLeod.
Douglas Maxwell.	Jimmy Shand.
Bill Morgan	Jimmy Lindsay
Archie Oliphant.	Jack Forsyth & Jimmy Shand.
Doug Proctor.	Highland Country Band.
Edd Robb.	Adam Rennie.
Stan Saunders.	Andrew Rankine, Jimmy Shand, Ian Holmes & Hamish Menzies.
Andrew "Sonny" Scott.	Peter White.
John Sinton	Jim MacLeod
Wiam Skinner.	Bobby Crowe & Jack Forsyth.
Monty Smillie	Alex MacArthur
Bert Smith.	Ian Powrie & Ian Arnott.
Norman Smith	Fraser McGlynn
John Strachan	Jimmy Shand
Maurice Thomson.	Alasdair Downie.

Willie Turner.

Dave Waters

John White.

Gordon Young.

John Johnstone.

Highland Country Band

Winifred Bird Matthew, Angus Fitchet, Jimmy Shand & Heather Scottish Dance Band.

Max Houliston.

Dave Barclay (Bass)

Dave Barclay from Friockham has been a great stalwart of the Scottish dance band scene, having played with Jack Forsyth, Lyndsay Ross, Jimmy Shand, Ian Powrie, Jimmy Blue and Bobby Crowe. A fine exponent of the double bass, Dave had a busy schedule with the bands of Ian Powrie and Jimmy Blue during the sixties and seventies. This involved broadcasting (radio and television), dances, theatre and tours abroad.

Stan Saunders (Bass)

Stan Saunders from Alloa has been involved in the Scottish dance music scene for over 40 years. A fine exponent of the bass fiddle, Stan has played with Andrew Rankine, Jimmy Shand, Ian Holmes and Hamish Menzies.

Drummers

Drummer	Band
Jimmy Bain	Wick Scottish Dance Band
Billy Black.	Angus Fitchet.
George Boath	Highland Country Band
Lawrence Brotherstone.	Bobby MacLeod.
Bobby Colgan.	Jim Johnstone, Ian Holmes, Alex MacArthur, Jimmy Shand & Jimmy Blue
Jack Cooper.	Jack Forsyth, Jimmy Blue & the Betty Anderson Quartet.
George Coutts.	Allan Williams Trio.
Watty Crole.	The Glendaruel Scottish Dance Band.
Bert Crow.	The Tayside Scottish Dance Band.
Drew Dalgleish.	Jim Johnstone & Max Houliston.
George Darling.	Andrew Rankine.
Alex Doig.	Jim MacLeod.
Bob Doig.	Jimmy Lindsay.
Bob Drylie.	Andrew Rankine.
Chris Duncan.	The Wick Scottish Dance Band.
Willie Duthie.	The Highland Country Band.
Arthur Easson.	Ian Powrie & Jimmy Blue.
Sandy Fearn.	The Blue Bonnets Scottish Dance Band.
Johnny Fellows.	Bobby MacLeod & Andrew Rankine.
Angus Fitchet Junior.	Jim Grogan.
Billy Ford.	Bobby MacLeod & Alasdair Downie.
Sandy Ford.	The Highland Country Band.
Tommy Gatherum.	Jack Forsyth.
David Glass.	The Gie Gordon Scottish Dance Band.
Bill Grant.	Lindsay Ross & Alex MacArthur.
John Gunn	Wick Scottish Dance Band
Andy Hamilton.	Andrew Rankine.
Ron Howie.	The Blue Bonnets Scottish Dance Band.
Bill Jarvis.	Jack Forsyth.
George Kessack.	Ian Mearns.
Colin Lander.	Bobby Crowe & the Olympians.
Bert Leishman.	Ian Holmes & Hamish Menzies.
Bill Mackie.	Peter White.
Owen McCabe.	Jimmy Shand.
Angus McDonald.	The Olympians.
Tom McDonald.	Hawthorne Accordion Band.
Ian McDougall.	Bobby MacLeod & Ian Holmes.

Dick McGill.	Alasdair Downie & Bobby MacLeod.
Hugh McIntyre.	Ian Powrie.
Jackie McLeod.	Fraser McGlynn.
Alex McMullen.	Jim MacLeod.
Gus Millar.	Hamish Menzies, Ian Holmes & Andrew Rankine.
Jimmy Miller.	The Mansfield Scottish Dance Quartet.
Billy Nelson.	Allan Williams Trio & Alex MacArthur.
Freddie Nicholson.	Murray MacKillop.
Norrie Ower.	The Cameron Kerr Scottish Dance Band.
Stan Peacock.	Ian Powrie & Jimmy Lindsay.
Steve Redpath.	Max Houliston.
Drew Robertson.	The Hamefarers.
Tommy Robertson.	The Olympians Scottish Dance Band.
Willie Robertson.	Fraser McGlynn.
Malcolm Ross	Bobby Crowe
Tom Shorthouse	Bert Shorthouse Quintet
Gordon Smith	Highland Country Band
Stan Spiers.	Ian Arnott.
Alasdair Stewart	Alex MacArthur
Willie Tervit.	The Arthur MacLeod Trio.
Billy Thom.	Andrew Rankine, Jim Johnstone & Jim MacLeod.
Jim Thornton	The Heather Scottish Dance Band
Henry Webster.	Jim Cameron.
Ally Wilkie.	The Highland Country Band & Jimmy Lindsay.
Willie Wilkie.	John Johnstone.
Ian Wilson	Jimmy Shand
Gordon Young.	Ian Holmes & Jim Johnstone.

Drummers

Here is a photograph of a group of four popular drummers, all of whom are fine exponents of the art of percussion. **Billy Thom** broadcast with Andrew Rankine, Jim Johnstone and Jim MacLeod. **Ian Wilson** with Jimmy Shand. **Jack Cooper** with Jack Forsyth, the Betty Anderson Quartet and Jimmy Blue. **Gus Millar** with Andrew Rankine, Hamish Menzies and Ian Holmes.

The foregoing serves to portray the rise in popularity of the bands which provided Scottish dance music in the peak years from 1945 until 1970. During that period I placed the band leaders in two categories - The Old Masters and The Young Masters.

The Old Masters were band leaders like Jimmy Shand, Bobby MacLeod, Jim Cameron, Ian Powrie, Angus Fitchet, Alasdair Downie, Jim MacLeod, Lindsay Ross and all of the other leaders that broadcast up to 1960. They set the mould for Scottish dance bands of the future. Albeit, they were not all technical wizards, many were self-taught, but everyone of them projected a big message with their music.

The Young Masters came on the scene in 1961. Band leaders like Bobby Crowe, Ian Holmes, Jim Johnstone, Max Houliston, Alex MacArthur, Fraser McGlynn and many more. Most had played with the earlier bands and were now sending out the same message with their style of music after having served their apprenticeship with the Old Masters.

Today, we still have many fine bands among the younger leaders, and with the drive and enthusiasm of that excellent BBC presenter, Robbie Shepherd, Scottish dance music still remains popular. With the Scottish dance music scene in such safe hands, I am sure that in the future, on a Saturday evening, people will still ask "Who's On The Dance Music Tonight".